THE EASTER STORY

Text by Deborah Lock

Illustrations © 2023 Friends & Heroes Productions Ltd

This edition copyright © 2023 Lion Hudson IP Limited

Published by **Candle Books**

www.lionhudson.com

Part of the SPCK Group

SPCK, 36 Causton Street, London, SW1P 4ST

ISBN 978 1 78128 419 3

First edition 2023

Acknowledgments

A catalogue record for this book is available from the British Library

Produced on paper from sustainable sources

Printed and bound in China, October 2022, LH54

THE EASTER STORY

CANDLE
BOOKS

Jesus and two of his disciples looked ahead at the city of Jerusalem. Jesus knew that the time had come to complete the work that God had given him to do. There was danger ahead for him; but Jesus trusted God, and a day of great glory was to come.

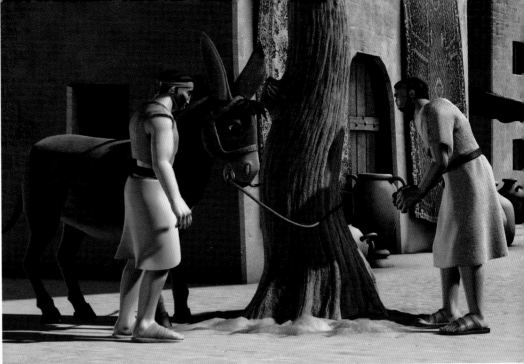

"Go ahead to the village nearby," Jesus told his friends. "You will find a young donkey that has never been ridden. Untie the colt and bring it to me. If anyone asks what you are doing, say, 'The Lord needs it and will return it.'" The friends did as Jesus asked.

When the disciples returned with the colt, they threw their cloaks over it. Jesus climbed on and rode into Jerusalem. Many others were heading toward Jerusalem because it was nearly time for the Jewish people to celebrate the Passover festival.

When the people saw Jesus, they knew he was the man who had said and done amazing things. Jesus had healed people with the power of God and he had told them about God's kingdom. They believed he was God's promised king that the ancient prophets said would come to them.

The crowd cut down leafy branches and laid them on the road. They cheered and waved, shouting, "Hosanna! Blessed is the king who comes in the name of God. God's kingdom is coming! Hosanna!"

When Jesus and his disciples entered Jerusalem, they went to the Temple. This was the most important place to the Jewish people. They went there to pray and make offerings to God in worship.

In the outer courtyard were the traders who exchanged money for Temple coins and those who sold doves and animals for offerings. The traders cheated the people. This made Jesus angry.

"This is a house of prayer and you have made it a den of robbers!" he cried, as he tipped over the tables, sending money scattering everywhere. The priests were afraid because Jesus was challenging their position and the people were supporting him.

They plotted to find a way to get rid of him.

The next day, Jesus and his disciples returned to the Temple.

Crowds gathered around Jesus, while Roman soldiers stood nearby making sure there was no trouble. Some religious leaders came to trap him with a question.

"Teacher," they asked, "we know that you speak truthfully about God's way and treat everybody alike. Tell us, is it right to pay taxes to the Roman governor or not?"

Jesus asked for a coin, and said, "Whose head is on this coin?"

"The emperor's," replied the men.

"Give back to the emperor what belongs to him," Jesus said, "and give back to God what belongs to God." Everyone was amazed at the wisdom of his answer. The religious leaders could not get him into trouble.

The Passover meal celebrates the time when God rescued the ancestors of the Jewish people from slavery in Egypt.

On the evening of the Passover meal, Jesus and his twelve disciples gathered in an upper room of a house. The meal was set out for them. Jesus knew that this was to be his last supper with them.

As his friends sat, Jesus took off his robe and tied a towel around his waist. He then poured water into a bowl and began to clean their hot and dusty feet. The disciples wondered why he was doing this rather than a servant.

Peter said, "Lord, you will never wash my feet."

Jesus replied, "If I do not, you will not belong to me."

Peter said eagerly, "Then wash my hands and my head, not just my feet."

Jesus shook his head and tried to explain, "Only your feet are dirty. Just as I have done, you should serve one another."

Jesus and the disciples began to eat.

"One of you will betray me," Jesus said as he passed a bowl to Judas, and they both dipped their bread into it. The other disciples declared that they would never let him down. Afterward Judas slipped away unnoticed.

Jesus then did something new. He picked up a piece of bread, gave thanks to God, and broke it. As he shared the pieces, he said, "I am giving up myself for you. Eat this to remember me."

At the end of the meal, Jesus took the cup of wine, gave thanks to God, and then passed it to his friends. He said, "I am going to die. Drink this to remember me, then people everywhere will know that God loves them."

After the meal, Jesus and his disciples sang a song of praise to God. Then they went out to a quiet garden of olive trees outside the city. On the way, Jesus warned his friends that they would be scared and leave him.

"The others may do that," said Peter, "but I will not."

Jesus replied, "Peter, this very night before dawn and the rooster crows, you will have said three times that you do not know me."

Peter shook his head, "Never! I will die with you before I say I don't know you." The others agreed.

When they reached the garden, Jesus went a little further with Peter, James, and John. He asked them to keep watch while he prayed.

In the darkness, Jesus prayed to God, "Abba, Father. You can do anything. Let me not suffer. But I will do as you want, and not what I want."

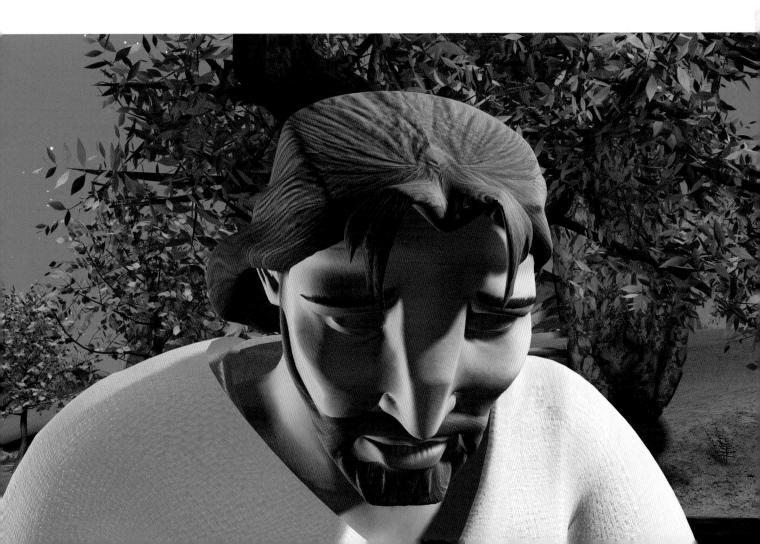

Jesus found his friends asleep each time he came back from praying. On the third time, Jesus heard a noise and woke them. A crowd sent by the chief priests came with swords and clubs, and Judas led them.

Judas said, "Rabbi, teacher," and kissed Jesus. The Temple soldiers arrested Jesus and dragged him away to the house of the high priest. There, Jesus was questioned by the Jewish Council.

Jesus' disciples fled, except for Peter who followed a little way behind. He crept into the courtyard of the house, but he was seen by the servants. They said,

"You were with Jesus!"

"You followed Jesus!"

"You came from Galilee with Jesus."

Each time, Peter denied knowing Jesus.

Then, the rooster crowed.

The Jewish Council accused Jesus of calling himself God's promised king. They wanted him executed, but only the Roman governor, Pilate, had the power to order this. The Council told Pilate that Jesus was causing trouble. Jesus stayed silent.

At this time each year, the governor could release any prisoner the people asked for. They had to choose between a rebel named Barabbas and Jesus.

Shouting wildly, the crowds cried, "Give us Barabbas!" Looking at Jesus, they shouted, "Crucify him!"

Pilate released Barabbas to keep the crowd happy. Then Jesus was taken away by the soldiers to be hung on a cross. The soldiers mocked Jesus, placing a purple cloak around him and a crown of thorns on his head.

"Hail! King of the Jews!" laughed the soldiers.

As Jesus hung from the cross, people jeered at him. A sign above his head read, "The King of the Jews". They laughed, "He saved others, but he does not save himself! Let him come down from the cross so that we may believe."

Darkness fell over the land even though it was the middle of the day. At three o'clock in the afternoon, Jesus cried out, "My God, my God. Why have you abandoned me?" A soldier lifted a sponge soaked in wine to Jesus' lips. Those watching wondered if Jesus would be rescued. Then Jesus gave a loud cry and died.

In the evening, Jesus' body was taken down and wrapped in linen cloth. He was buried in a tomb and a great stone door was rolled over the entrance.

On the third day after Jesus' death, two of Jesus' friends were walking from Jerusalem to the village of Emmaus. As they chatted, a stranger joined them.

"What are you discussing?" the stranger asked.

"All that happened to our friend Jesus," they replied sadly. "He did great deeds and spoke God's word, but he was crucified. Some women have shocked us this morning. Jesus' body has gone, and they say he is alive."

The stranger said, "Why do you not believe? Don't you understand God's promised king had to suffer to complete God's work and enter glory? The Jewish writings explain this."

At Emmaus, the stranger stayed for supper. He picked up the bread, gave thanks and broke it. Suddenly, Jesus' friends knew the stranger to be Jesus, but at that moment he was gone.

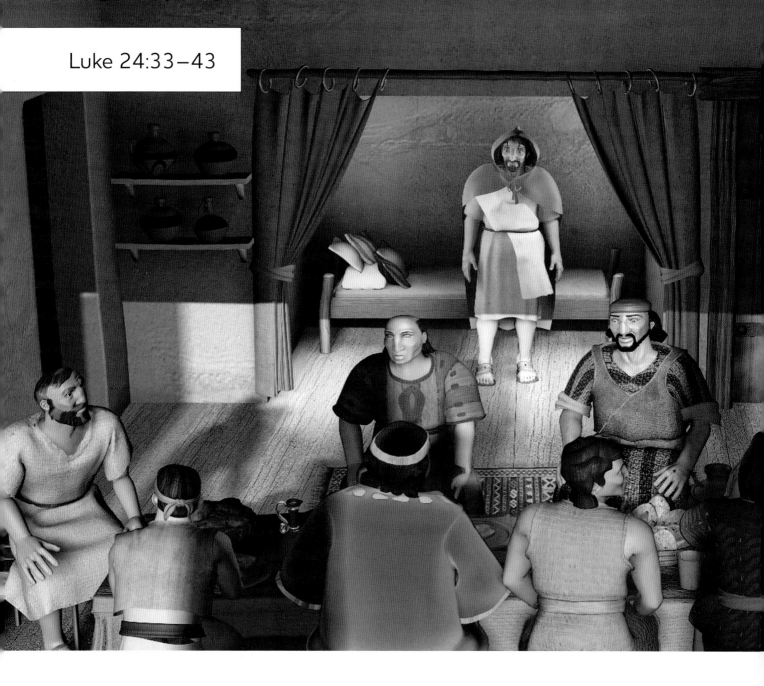

The two friends rushed back to Jerusalem to tell the other disciples. As they told them the news, Jesus appeared in the room. The disciples thought he was a ghost.

"Peace be with you," Jesus said. "Do not be afraid. Touch me and see." Jesus showed them the marks from the nails of the cross on his hands and his feet. The disciples were full of joy and wonder.

"Have you anything to eat?" Jesus asked. They gave him some fish. As he ate, Jesus talked to them. "You are witnesses of who I am, God's promised king."

Jesus blessed them, and the disciples praised him.

Let's chat!

1. What did Jesus ride to enter Jerusalem?
    a. A horse
    b. A camel
    c. A young donkey

2. What did Jesus do to show the disciples how to serve one another?
    a. He set the table.
    b. He washed their feet.
    c. He cleaned the dishes.

3. What was written on the sign above Jesus' head on the cross?
    a. The King of the Jews
    b. Rebel leader
    c. Thief

4. How did Jesus' friends recognize Jesus at Emmaus?
    a. Jesus sang a hymn.
    b. Jesus took the bread, gave thanks, and broke it.
    c. Jesus was wearing the same clothes as before.

5. Which two things helped the disciples know that Jesus was not a ghost?

a. He showed them his hands and feet.

b. Jesus suddenly appeared.

c. Jesus ate some fish.

- Which part of the Easter story do you like best?

- What makes the Easter story special for you?

- What do you think is the most important message about the Easter story?

Also available

Friends and Heroes Bible

Friends and Heroes The Nativity Story

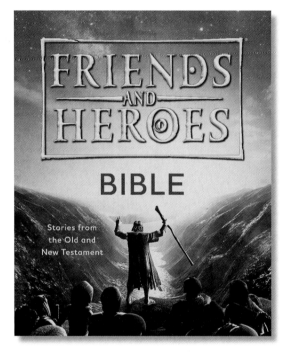

978 1 78128 420 9

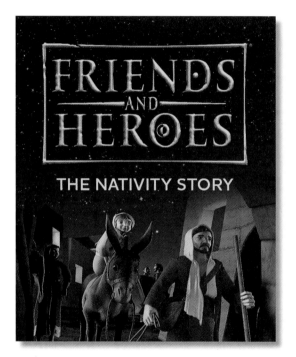

978 1 78128 416 2